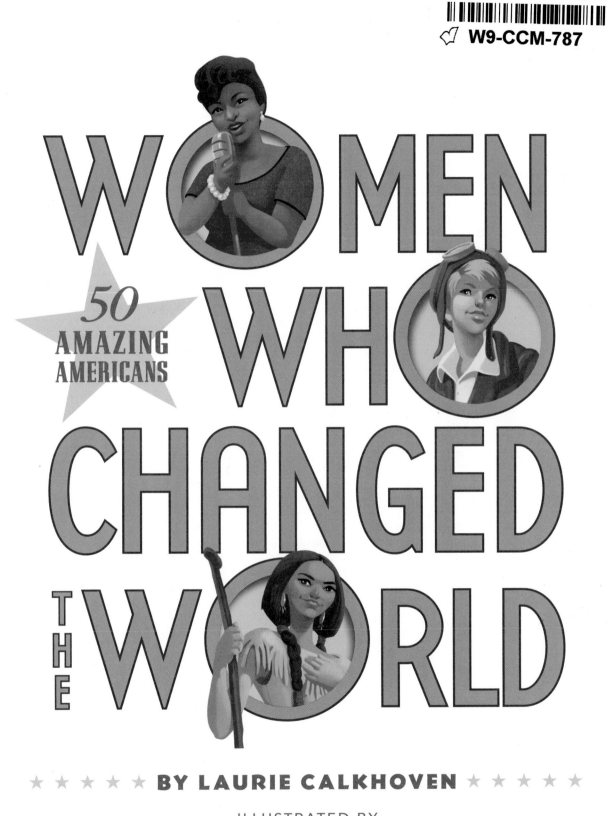

WOMEN WHO CHANGED THE WORLD

50 AMAZING AMERICANS

★ ★ ★ ★ ★ BY LAURIE CALKHOVEN ★ ★ ★ ★ ★

ILLUSTRATED BY

★ ★ ★ ★ ★ PATRICIA CASTELAO ★ ★ ★ ★ ★

Scholastic Inc.

For the first amazing woman in my life,
Shirley Calkhoven, who showed me that women can do anything. -LC

For my little girl, Claudia, who enjoyed this project as much as I did. -PC

Text Copyright © 2016 by Laurie Calkhoven.
Illustration Copyright © 2016 by Scholastic Inc.

All rights reserved. Published by Scholastic Inc., *Publishers since 1920*.
SCHOLASTIC and associated logos are trademarks and/or registered trademarks of Scholastic Inc.

The publisher does not have any control over and does not assume any responsibility for author or third-party websites or their content.

No part of this work may be reproduced, stored in a retrieval system, or transmitted in any form or by any means, electronic, mechanical, photocopying, recording, or otherwise, without written permission of the publisher. For information regarding permission, write to Scholastic Inc., Attention: Permissions Department, 557 Broadway, New York, NY 10012.

Library of Congress Cataloging-in-Publication Data available.

ISBN 978-0-545-88962-9

10 9 8 7 6 5 4   16 17 18 19 20

Printed in the U.S.A.   40
First edition, 2016
Book design by Elliot Kreloff

★ ★ ★ ★ ★ ★ ★ ★ ★ TABLE OF CONTENTS ★ ★ ★ ★ ★ ★ ★ ★ ★

Introduction   **5**

POCAHONTAS (c.1595–1617): *Peacemaker*   **6**

ABIGAIL ADAMS (1744–1818): *First Lady, Advocate for Women's Rights*   **8**

SACAGAWEA (c.1788–1812): *Explorer*   **10**

SOJOURNER TRUTH (1797–1883): *Abolitionist*   **12**

ELIZABETH CADY STANTON (1815–1902): *Women's Rights Advocate*   **14**

SUSAN B. ANTHONY (1820–1906): *Women's Rights Advocate*   **15**

ELIZABETH BLACKWELL (1821–1910): *Doctor*   **16**

CLARA BARTON (1821–1912): *Founder of the American Red Cross*   **18**

HARRIET TUBMAN (c.1822–1913): *Freedom Fighter*   **20**

EMILY DICKINSON (1830–1886): *Poet*   **22**

LOUISA MAY ALCOTT (1832–1888): *Author*   **23**

JANE ADDAMS (1860–1935): *Activist*   **24**

JULIETTE GORDON LOW (1860–1927): *Founder of the Girl Scouts*   **25**

ANNIE JUMP CANNON (1863–1941): *Astronomer*   **26**

NELLIE BLY (1864–1922): *Groundbreaking Journalist*   **28**

LAURA INGALLS WILDER (1867–1957): *Pioneer Author*   **30**

HELEN KELLER (1880–1968): *Humanitarian*   **32**

ELEANOR ROOSEVELT (1884–1962): *First Lady, Champion of Human Rights*   **34**

GEORGIA O'KEEFFE (1887–1986): *Artist*   **36**

AMELIA EARHART (1897–1937): *Aviator*   **38**

MARGARET MEAD (1901–1978): *Trailblazing Anthropologist*   **40**

MARGARET BOURKE-WHITE (1904–1971): *Pioneering Photojournalist*   **41**

RACHEL CARSON (1907–1964): *Environmentalist*   **42**

BABE DIDRIKSON ZAHARIAS (1911–1956): *Athlete*   **44**

LUCILLE BALL (1911–1989): *Comedian*   **46**

JULIA CHILD (1912–2004): *Chef*   48

ROSA PARKS (1913–2005): *Civil Rights Activist*   50

BARBARA MCCLINTOCK (1902–1992): *Geneticist*   52

GERTRUDE ELION (1918–1999): *Pharmacologist*   53

ELLA FITZGERALD (1918–1996): *Jazz Singer*   54

NANCY REAGAN (1921–): *First Lady, Anti-Drug Activist*   56

MARIA TALLCHIEF (1925–2013): *Ballerina*   58

BARBARA BUSH (1925–): *First Lady, Literacy Advocate*   60

CORETTA SCOTT KING (1927–2006): *Civil Rights Activist*   62

PATSY TAKEMOTO MINK (1927–2002): *Congresswoman*   64

MAYA ANGELOU (1928–2014): *Author*   66

HARPER LEE (1926–): *Novelist*   68

BARBARA WALTERS (1929–): *Journalist*   69

DIAN FOSSEY (1932–1985): *Zoologist*   70

GLORIA STEINEM (1934–): *Feminist*   72

HILLARY RODHAM CLINTON (1947–): *Politician*   74

SALLY RIDE (1951–2012): *Astronaut*   76

OPRAH WINFREY (1954–): *Media Mogul*   78

SONIA SOTOMAYOR (1954–): *Supreme Court Justice*   80

CONDOLEEZZA RICE (1954–): *Secretary of State*   82

ANN BANCROFT (1955–): *Polar Explorer*   84

MAYA LIN (1959–): *Artist and Architect*   86

MICHELLE OBAMA (1964–): *First Lady, Children's Health Advocate*   88

SERENA WILLIAMS (1981–): *Tennis Star*   90

MISTY COPELAND (1982–): *Ballerina*   92

More Amazing Women Who Changed the World   94

Glossary   96

WOMEN have always played an important role in the history of the United States. But before they were women, they were girls. And they were just like you and me. They liked to swim and listen to music, read, and hang out with their friends. Seemingly ordinary girls grew up to be extraordinary women!

The women you'll meet in this book all have different stories to tell. Some of them, like Harriet Tubman and Sojourner Truth, were born into slavery and grew up to fight for freedom. Elizabeth Blackwell had a love of science that led her to become the first female doctor in the country, and Dian Fossey spent eighteen years studying gorillas in Africa. Some women fought for equal rights for all people, or for women's right to vote. And some, like Amelia Earhart and Sally Ride, proved to everyone that women could do anything that men could do.

All of them grew up to change the world in some way, and we have them to thank for making our country a stronger, more exciting, and better place for all people to live in today. Turn the page to be inspired by their stories, and you, too, can grow up to change the world!

POCAHONTAS

FACT FILE

★ **BORN:** Around 1595, near present-day Jamestown, Virginia

★ **SPOUSE:** John Rolfe

★ **CHILDREN:** Thomas

★ **DIED:** March 21, 1617, in Gravesend, England

Pocahontas was a Native American princess. Her father was chief of more than thirty Powhatan Indian tribes. Powhatan women and girls farmed and built houses. They also made pottery, wove baskets, and stitched beadwork. At night there was music and dancing. Pocahontas loved to dance!

In 1607, a group of Englishmen founded a settlement on the banks of the James River. The **settlers** struggled to find food, and many died. One settler, John Smith, was captured by the Powhatans. He was about to be put to death when Pocahontas, who didn't want to see him hurt, saved his life.

Pocahontas started to visit Jamestown. She and Smith learned to speak each other's languages, and she kept the **colonists** alive with gifts of food. She also warned Smith when her father planned to attack, saving his life for a second time.

PLAYFUL ONE

Pocahontas's real name was Matoaka. Her father nicknamed her Pocahontas, which means "playful one." She loved to laugh and dance and sing.

Smith sailed back to England, and Pocahontas didn't visit the settlers for many years. Then, in 1613, she was taken prisoner by the English, who wanted to negotiate with her father. Her father refused, so Pocahontas continued to live with the settlers. One man, John Rolfe, fell in love with her and asked her to marry him. She said yes, and together they had a son named Thomas.

PEACEMAKER

THE POCAHONTAS PEACE

After Pocahontas married John Rolfe, there was a new peace between the English settlers and the Powhatans. This friendship, known as the Peace of Pocahontas, lasted for many years.

In May 1616, she sailed with her small family to England, where Pocahontas was presented to the British king and queen. She was a star in London society.

About a year later, the family boarded a ship to return home. They hadn't gone far when Pocahontas became ill, and she died soon after.

ABIGAIL ADAMS

Abigail Adams grew up in a home surrounded by farms and forest. Like other girls of her time, she didn't go to school. She was taught to read and write at home, and enjoyed reading many of the books in her minister father's library. She also learned how to cook, sew, and do needlework.

When she first met a twenty-three-year-old lawyer named John Adams, fourteen-year-old Abigail thought he talked too much. But she got to know him better and learned they had a lot in common. A few years later, she married him.

John got involved in local and then national politics when the colonists became unhappy with the way the British government was treating them. John's work often kept him away from home, so Abigail managed the farm and raised their children. When she didn't travel with John, they exchanged letters.

WAR WORK

Abigail watched the Battle of Bunker Hill from a peak near her home. John was away in Philadelphia, but Abigail took in people who were escaping from the British, and melted pewter plates and utensils to make bullets for the American soldiers.

She sent one of her most famous letters when John was in Philadelphia working on the Constitution for the new country. At the time, women had very few legal rights. Abigail urged her husband to "remember the ladies," and to make laws that were generous to women. It would be many years, however, before women could own property and vote.

FIRST LADY, ADVOCATE FOR WOMEN'S RIGHTS

EDUCATION FOR GIRLS

Abigail was embarrassed by her lack of education, and especially by her bad spelling and poor handwriting. She thought girls should have the same education as boys, and argued that educated mothers raised more intelligent children.

John Adams became president in 1797. He discussed the problems of the country with Abigail and she often gave him advice. Many people thought she had too much power and called her "Mrs. President."

When John lost to Thomas Jefferson in his second election, Abigail was happy to go home to Massachusetts. She led a peaceful life surrounded by children and grandchildren.

SACAGAWEA

Sacagawea, the daughter of a Shoshone Indian chief, was born in what is now Idaho. We know almost nothing about her early years. When she was twelve years old, she was kidnapped by a war party of Hidatsa Indians. They took her to North Dakota and sold her to Toussaint Charbonneau, a French-Canadian fur trader who made Sacagawea one of his wives.

In November 1804, the Lewis and Clark **expedition** (see sidebar) built a fort near the Hidatsa village where Sacagawea lived. Lewis and Clark needed Shoshone horses to cross the Bitterroot Mountains. They thought Sacagawea could be helpful to them when it came time to trade with the Shoshone.

LEWIS AND CLARK EXPEDITION

In 1803, President Thomas Jefferson asked Meriwether Lewis to lead an expedition across western North America. Lewis's co-leader was William Clark. Their job was to map the rivers, make friends with Native Americans, and look for an easy water route from the east coast to the west coast.

Sacagawea gave birth to her son, Jean-Baptiste Charbonneau, in the American fort on February 11, 1805. With her baby on her back, Sacagawea became the only woman to join the expedition.

In August, the expedition found a band of Shoshone. Their leader was Sacagawea's brother. After their emotional reunion, Sacagawea helped Lewis and Clark negotiate with her brother and the tribe to buy the horses they needed.

EXPLORER

SACAGAWEA'S ROLE

Sacagawea was an important member of the expedition. Native American tribes became friendly when they saw her, because war parties never traveled with women. She also collected plants and picked berries for food and medicine.

In November 1805, the expedition reached the Pacific Ocean. On the journey home, Sacagawea led the group on Shoshone trails she remembered from her childhood.

The expedition returned to Sacagawea's Hidatsa village on August 14, 1806. She was paid nothing for her work. Her husband was given $500.33 and 320 acres of land.

Six years later, in August 1812, Sacagawea gave birth to a daughter, Lisette. When Sacagawea died four months later, William Clark adopted her two children.

A GAME OF TELEPHONE

Sacagawea spoke Shoshone and Hidatsa. Her husband spoke Hidatsa and French. Another member of the party spoke French and English. He made the final translations for Captains Lewis and Clark!

SOJOURNER TRUTH

FACT FILE

★ **BORN:** November 1797, in Ulster County, New York

★ **SPOUSE:** Thomas

★ **CHILDREN:** Diana, Peter, Elizabeth, Sophia, and a possible fifth child

★ **DIED:** November 26, 1883, in Battle Creek, Michigan

Sojourner Truth was born a slave named Isabella Baumfree. Her mother had twelve other children, most of whom were sold to different owners. Sojourner herself was sold away from her parents when she was nine. Her master was cruel and often hit her. She slept in a cold, dark basement. Eventually, she was sold to a new owner named John Dumont.

MEETING PRESIDENT LINCOLN

During the Civil War, Sojourner led efforts to provide food, education, and employment to ex-slaves. In 1864, she met with President Abraham Lincoln to discuss the future of those newly free people. She described Lincoln as a "great and good man . . . [who treated her] with great kindness and **cordiality**."

Sojourner spent seventeen years with the Dumont family. She married another slave named Thomas and had five children. When a law was passed that would have freed her, Sojourner's owner refused to let her go, so she ran away with her only child who had not been sold. Later, she successfully fought to get back her son Peter, who had been sold to an owner in Alabama.

Sojourner had religious visions, including one that urged her to change her name to Sojourner Truth. She began to travel around the North, preaching. Whites and blacks came together to hear her speak. Sojourner worked with other **abolitionists** and spoke out against slavery. She was also an **advocate** for women's rights.

★ ABOLITIONIST

WHAT'S IN A NAME?

"Sojourner" means traveler. Sojourner Truth was the perfect name for someone who traveled from town to town to speak the truth.

Sojourner never stopped fighting for rights for black men and for all women. She died at the age of eighty-six, still speaking out for freedom and equality for all.

SOJOURNER ON MARS

NASA named a Mars Rover after Sojourner Truth. The small robot landed on Mars aboard the *Pathfinder* spacecraft on July 4, 1997. *Sojourner* set out to take pictures, perform science experiments, and send information back to Earth. The vehicle is still "sojourning" on the surface of the red planet!

ELIZABETH CADY STANTON

WOMEN'S RIGHTS ADVOCATE

FACT FILE

★ **BORN:** November 12, 1815, in Johnstown, New York
★ **SPOUSE:** Henry Stanton
★ **CHILDREN:** Daniel, Henry, Gerrit, Theodore, Margaret, Harriot, Robert
★ **DIED:** October 26, 1902, in New York, New York

Elizabeth Cady was born in a world that thought boys were better than girls. When her brother died in 1826, she tried to cheer up her father by becoming more boyish. He allowed her to study subjects like Greek that were normally reserved for boys, but she could not replace her brother in his eyes.

She studied in her father's law office and saw the problems women faced. They couldn't inherit property or sign contracts. Everything they had belonged to their fathers or their husbands. And perhaps most important, women couldn't vote.

Elizabeth decided to do something to improve the lives of women. In 1848, she brought women together in Seneca Falls, New York, to talk about the problems they faced. If women could vote, Elizabeth knew they could work to change other laws. Three years later, she teamed up with Susan B. Anthony (see page 15) to lead the fight for women's **suffrage**.

In 1920, eighteen years after Elizabeth's death, the Nineteenth Amendment was passed, granting American women the right to vote.

SENECA FALLS CONVENTION AND THE DECLARATION OF SENTIMENTS

In 1848, Elizabeth and her friend Lucretia Mott organized a convention in Seneca Falls, New York, to talk about women's rights. Elizabeth presented the Declaration of **Sentiments**, which she had written and modeled on the Declaration of Independence. It called for women to be treated equally in law and in society. The convention marked the beginning of the women's suffrage movement in the United States.

SUSAN B. ANTHONY

FACT FILE

★ **BORN:** February 15, 1820, in Adams, Massachusetts

★ **SPOUSE:** Never married

★ **CHILDREN:** None

★ **DIED:** March 13, 1906, in Rochester, New York

Like Elizabeth Cady Stanton, Susan B. Anthony worked to end slavery. She was also involved in the temperance movement, an effort to ban alcohol. When she stood up to speak at a convention, she was told that women were not allowed to talk. That led her to become involved in the women's rights movement.

Susan had been raised in a Quaker family. Their religion saw women as equal to men. When she became a teacher in New York, she learned that male teachers were paid much more than female teachers. She asked for equal pay, and lost her job.

From the moment Susan met Elizabeth in 1851, they became a strong team. Elizabeth often wrote the speeches, while Susan, who was a better speaker, delivered them. She would babysit for Elizabeth's seven children, so that her friend had the time to write.

Susan spent thirty years traveling around the country speaking up for women's rights. In her very last speech, she said, "Failure is impossible."

She was right. Women earned the right to vote on August 18, 1920—fourteen years after her death.

UNDER ARREST

Susan was arrested after voting in a presidential election in 1872, casting her ballot for Ulysses S. Grant. At her trial, a judge found her guilty of voting illegally and fined her $100, which would be almost $2,000 today!

ELIZABETH BLACKWELL

Elizabeth Blackwell's parents believed in equal rights for women. She and her four sisters had the same education as their four brothers. When her father's business failed, Elizabeth and her family moved from England to America. They first settled in New York City and then moved to Ohio.

When Elizabeth's father died, she and her two older sisters opened a boarding school in their home to support the family. Once the family's finances improved, Elizabeth was free to pursue her own dreams. A sick friend told Elizabeth that she would have been happier with a female doctor. That gave Elizabeth an idea—why couldn't she be a doctor? She worked to earn money for medical school, and in 1847, she sent out applications. Every school turned her down except for one—New York's Geneva Medical College. Elizabeth became the first female medical student in U.S. history.

A PRACTICAL JOKE

Geneva Medical College left the decision about Elizabeth's application to the students, sure that the young men would say no. As a joke, the students voted to allow her to enroll. But the joke was on them when Elizabeth arrived a few weeks later and worked harder than most of the male students to keep her place.

DOCTOR

CHANGING PEOPLE'S MINDS

When Elizabeth first tried to set up her medical practice in New York City, landlords wouldn't rent to her, men shouted insults, and women crossed the street to avoid her. After she began to treat poor women and children for free, opinions about female doctors started to change.

Elizabeth graduated with top honors. When she was ready to set up a medical practice, she returned to New York City. Many patients didn't trust a female doctor, so she opened a free infirmary for poor women and children. It was so popular that she then opened a hospital.

For the rest of her life, Elizabeth treated poor women and children and was a champion of women's rights.

CLARA BARTON

FACT FILE

★ **BORN:** December 25, 1821, in Oxford, Massachusetts

★ **SPOUSE:** Never married

★ **CHILDREN:** None

★ **DIED:** April 12, 1912, in Glen Echo, Maryland

Clarissa Barton was born on Christmas Day. The family nicknamed her Clara, and the shy girl grew up doing farm chores such as milking cows, feeding chickens, and gathering eggs. Clara had four older siblings. Her sister Dolly taught her to read. Stephen and Sally taught her other school subjects. And her brother David taught her how to throw a ball, use tools, and tie knots.

A family friend suggested that teaching would cure Clara's shyness. As a teen, Clara took over a one-room schoolhouse and became a good teacher. She taught for a number of years before moving to Washington, D.C., to become an office clerk, and she was there at the start of the Civil War.

When Clara learned that a group of Massachusetts soldiers had lost everything, she gathered supplies for them. She also volunteered in army hospitals. But she knew that she could save more lives if she was on the battlefield. The army said it would be too hard for a woman, but Clara finally got permission to be a battlefield nurse. The soldiers called her the "Angel of the Battlefield."

FIRST PATIENT

When she was eleven, Clara's brother David was badly hurt in a farm accident. Clara took care of David day and night. She gave him medicine and even applied leeches to his skin, which people mistakenly used to believe would remove whatever was causing the illness from a patient's body.

FOUNDER OF THE AMERICAN RED CROSS

FIRST AID

When Clara retired from the Red Cross in 1904, she started a new organization—the National First Aid Association of America. She taught people the correct first-aid treatments and encouraged every home in America to have a first-aid kit.

After the war, Clara traveled to Europe and learned about the International Red Cross, an organization that helped wounded soldiers and people who lost everything in natural disasters. She was so inspired by what she saw that she came home to start the Red Cross in America. Whenever there was a disaster like a flood or an earthquake, Clara led her volunteers to build shelters, feed the homeless, and give out **donations**.

Clara led the Red Cross for more than twenty years, bringing relief and hope to people all over the country.

HARRIET TUBMAN

FACT FILE

★ **BORN:** Around 1822, in Dorchester Country, Maryland

★ **SPOUSE:** John Tubman (1844–1867),

Nelson Davis (1869–1888)

★ **CHILDREN:** None

★ **DIED:** March 10, 1913, in Auburn, New York

Harriet Tubman was born a slave in late February or early March of 1820 or 1822. She soon became a babysitter for her younger siblings. When she was just five or six, she was taken away from her mother and hired out to a nearby slave master.

As a slave, Harriet was often beaten and nearly died more than once, but she still believed she could be free. Her brothers were too afraid to run away with her, so one dark night in 1849 she crept into the woods alone. She hid in swamps and forests as she traveled north and trusted strangers who could have turned her over to slave catchers. Days later, she crossed the border into Pennsylvania and was finally free.

A NEARLY DEADLY BLOW

One night in 1836, Harriet was trying to stand up for another slave when a white boss broke her skull with a heavy weight. Harriet was forced to work in the fields with blood pouring down her face. Somehow, she lived, but she had terrible headaches for the rest of her life.

But having her freedom wasn't enough for Harriet. She wanted her family to be free, too. She worked hard, saved her money, and made many trips back to the South to bring her family and other slaves to freedom. And when the Civil War broke out, she became a spy and scout for the Union army.

FREEDOM FIGHTER

UNDERGROUND RAILROAD

The Underground Railroad wasn't underground and it wasn't actually a railroad. It was a secret network of whites and free blacks that helped runaway slaves travel to freedom. Guides called themselves "conductors." Harriet Tubman was the most famous and most successful conductor on the Underground Railroad.

No one knows for sure how many slaves Harriet helped. Her work was too dangerous and had to be kept secret. But many years later she said, "I was the conductor on the Underground Railroad for eight years, and I can say what most conductors can't say—I never ran my train off the track and I never lost a passenger."

Harriet died in 1913 and was buried with full military honors. In 2015, she was the first choice of online voters to be the woman to replace Andrew Jackson as the face on the twenty-dollar bill. Perhaps one day soon we'll see a woman like Harriet on our money!

EMILY DICKINSON

POET

Emily Dickinson, perhaps the greatest American poet, led a quiet life in Amherst, Massachusetts. Like other girls, she learned how to take care of a house and a garden. She also played the piano, and loved reading and taking long walks.

When she was fifteen, Emily spent just one year away from home at a college called Mount Holyoke Female Seminary (now Mount Holyoke College). She soon returned home to Amherst, where she most liked to be. Her younger sister, Lavinia, and her sister-in-law, Susan, were her closest friends. When Emily was in her twenties, she began writing more.

When she wasn't in her garden or writing poetry, Emily took long walks in the hills around Amherst, always alone. By the late 1860s, she stopped leaving the house and garden altogether.

Not one of Emily's poems was published during her lifetime. After she died, her family discovered forty handmade books of almost 1,800 poems. Four years later, her first book of poetry was published. It was a huge success, and she remains one of America's most beloved writers.

GREEN THUMB

Emily's love of gardening may have started with a school project when she created an herbarium, or collection of plants. She wrote to a friend: "Have you made an herbarium yet? I hope you will, if you have not, it would be such a treasure to you." She tended to the herbarium for the rest of her life.

LOUISA MAY ALCOTT — AUTHOR

FACT FILE

★ **BORN:** November 29, 1832, in Germantown, Philadelphia, Pennsylvania
★ **SPOUSE:** Never married
★ **CHILDREN:** None
★ **DIED:** March 6, 1888, in Boston, Massachusetts

Louisa May Alcott was born on her father's birthday. He was a **philosopher** and teacher, and he taught Louisa and her three sisters, Anna, Elizabeth, and May. Like the character Jo March in her famous novel *Little Women*, Louisa was a tomboy. She also loved to write.

The Alcotts struggled with poverty, and at the age of fifteen, Louisa decided to do something about it. For many years, she did whatever work she could find, like cleaning, sewing, teaching, and working as a **governess**. She also began selling her poems and stories to newspapers and magazines. Her first book, *Flower Fables*, was published when she was twenty-two. More books followed, but it wasn't until an editor asked her to write a story for girls that Louisa became truly successful. She wrote a novel based on growing up with her sisters, one of whom, Elizabeth, had recently died.

BLOOD AND THUNDER

Many of Louisa's newspaper stories were daring "blood and thunder" thrillers about murder and revenge. No one wanted to read stories like that by a woman, so she used the pen name A.M. Barnard.

Little Women brought Louisa fame and fortune. She followed it up with more books about the fictional March sisters, and used her earnings to take care of her parents. She died in 1888, just two days after her father.

JANE ADDAMS

ACTIVIST

FACT FILE

★ **BORN:** September 6, 1860, in Cedarville, Illinois

★ **SPOUSE:** Never married

★ **CHILDREN:** None

★ **DIED:** May 21, 1935, in Chicago, Illinois

Jane Addams's mother died when she was just two years old. Her father, a state senator and friend of Abraham Lincoln, fought against slavery. He inspired Jane to do good. She hoped to become a doctor, but her own poor health forced her to drop out of medical school.

Jane went to Europe to recover. After watching a bullfight and feeling sorry for the bull, she got the idea to create a home to help the poor. Jane cut her trip short and returned to Illinois to open Hull House in the middle of Chicago's poorest neighborhood in 1889. Hull House offered hot lunches, child care for working women, English classes, lectures, plays, concerts, and parties. The home helped hundreds of thousands of people.

In 1931, Jane became the first American woman to receive the Nobel Peace Prize, in recognition of her life-changing work.

PEACEMAKER

Jane spoke out for peace even when it was unpopular. Before World War I, she was one of the most respected women in America. When the United States entered the war, Jane continued to speak against it. Newspapers called her a traitor, but Jane stuck to her beliefs.

JULIETTE GORDON LOW

FOUNDER OF THE GIRL SCOUTS

FACT FILE

★ **BORN:** October 31, 1860, in Savannah, Georgia

★ **SPOUSE:** William Low

★ **CHILDREN:** None

★ **DIED:** January 17, 1927, in Savannah, Georgia

Juliette Gordon was her name, but everyone called her Daisy. Daisy loved animals and often took in stray cats and dogs. She liked listening to stories about her great-grandmother, who had been captured by Seneca Indians at the age of nine. And she loved outdoor adventures!

Daisy grew up and married William Low, but when her husband died, she found herself searching for something useful to do. When she met the founder of the Girl Guides in England, she discovered her calling. She came home and founded the Girl Guides of America, which today we know as the Girl Scouts of the USA.

The Girl Scouts urged girls to get outdoors and explore the world around them. The group also encouraged girls to be ready to take on roles as professional women, and even welcomed girls with disabilities at a time when that was unusual.

The first troop had eighteen members. The Girl Scouts has since grown to become the largest organization for girls and young women in the world.

HEADSTANDS

Juliette liked doing headstands. Every year on her birthday, she stood on her head to prove that she could still do it. Once, she even did a headstand at the national headquarters to show off her new Girl Scout shoes!

ANNIE JUMP CANNON

FACT FILE

★ **BORN:** December 11, 1863, in Dover, Delaware

★ **SPOUSE:** Never married

★ **CHILDREN:** None

★ **DIED:** April 13, 1941, in Cambridge, Massachusetts

Annie Jump Cannon's father was a shipbuilder and a state senator. It was her mother, Mary, who taught her the constellations and the names of the stars, from the rooftop of their home. Her mom encouraged Annie's interest in astronomy—the branch of science that deals with stars, planets, and space. Annie went to Wellesley College to study physics and astronomy and went on to Radcliffe College for advanced study.

In 1896, Annie became an assistant at the Harvard Observatory. She joined a team that was working to photograph and **classify** the stars. Annie came up with a simplified way to classify stars and planets, and her method was quickly adopted all over the world. It's still in use today! Annie studied hundreds of thousands of stars over the course of her career, discovering more than 300 new stars.

ECLIPSE

In 1892, Annie traveled to Europe to take pictures of an **eclipse** of the sun. A camera company printed a booklet of her photos called "In the Footsteps of Columbus" and sold it at the 1893 Chicago World's Fair.

ASTRONOMER

KISS ME!

Annie's system uses the letters O, B, A, F, G, K, M to classify the stars. For years, astronomers have used the sentence "Oh, Be A Fine Girl (or Guy)—Kiss Me!" to memorize the letters.

Her work was so well respected that she became the first woman to receive an honorary doctorate from the University of Oxford. She was also the first female officer in the American Astronomical Society.

Annie wanted everyone to be as enthusiastic about the stars as she was. She also wanted more girls to study astronomy. In 1933, she created the Annie Jump Cannon Award for female astronomers.

GOOGLE DOODLE

On what would have been her 151st birthday, December 11, 2014, Annie got an honor she never would have dreamed of—she was the Google doodle of the day! Everyone who visited the Google website saw a picture of Annie studying a star.

NELLIE BLY

Elizabeth Jane Cochran, known as Nellie Bly, grew up competing with two older brothers. She was nicknamed "Pink" because she loved to wear frilly pink dresses.

Nellie's father died when she was six and her mother struggled to support the family. At fifteen, Nellie went to school to be a teacher, but she couldn't afford to stay. When she read an article in a Pittsburgh newspaper that said working women were a "monstrosity," Nellie sent an angry letter to the editor. He hired her to be a reporter and gave her the pen name Nellie Bly.

After two years, Nellie moved to New York City and made a name for herself writing for the *New York World*. She wrote about the lives of ordinary women and the poor. Then she had an idea to take a trip around the world in less than eighty days and beat the record of Phileas Fogg (see sidebar). Nellie's editor said it couldn't be done, especially by a woman. She said if he didn't send her, she'd find a newspaper that would.

TEN DAYS IN A MADHOUSE

Nellie's first job for the *New York World* was to report on the Women's Lunatic Asylum in New York City. She had to pretend to be insane so that a judge would send her to the **asylum**. When the newspaper got her released ten days later, Nellie wrote about terrible beatings, freezing-cold baths, and rotten food. The story made Nellie famous.

GROUNDBREAKING JOURNALIST

AROUND THE WORLD IN EIGHTY DAYS

Nellie was trying to beat the record of a *fictional* character, not someone who had actually had an around-the-world adventure. Phileas Fogg was the hero of Jules Verne's popular novel *Around the World in Eighty Days*.

Nellie traveled by ship, by train, and even by donkey! On the last leg of her journey, crowds cheered, bands played, and fireworks lit the sky. Everyone wanted Nellie to beat the record—and she did. She made it back to New York in seventy-two days, six hours, and eleven minutes.

LAURA INGALLS WILDER

FACT FILE

★ BORN: February 7, 1867, near Pepin, Wisconsin

★ SPOUSE: Almanzo Wilder

★ CHILDREN: Rose Wilder Lane

★ DIED: February 10, 1957, in Mansfield, Missouri

Laura Ingalls was born in the big woods of Wisconsin. Her family—Pa, Ma, and big sister, Mary—lived in a log cabin. When Laura was two, they crossed the prairie in a covered wagon and settled in Kansas. They built a house and cleared land for a farm. Then they discovered that the land belonged to the Osage Indians, so they had to return to Wisconsin.

As girls, Laura and Mary churned butter, sewed quilts, washed dishes, and helped Ma with the housework. At night, Pa played his fiddle. Sometimes, they could hear wolves howling outside.

When Laura was seven, the family filled their covered wagon and set out for Minnesota. They settled on the banks of Plum Creek, near the town of Walnut Grove, where Laura and Mary went to school. Swarms of grasshoppers destroyed Pa's wheat crop and the family moved again, this time to run a hotel in Iowa. It was hard work and they missed the prairie. Two years later they left Iowa and settled in the Dakota Territory.

FALL TREATS

In Wisconsin, Laura and the other children looked forward to a once-a-year treat—roasted pig tail! Pigs were roasted in the fall so families would have meat for the winter.

PIONEER AUTHOR

MARY'S EYES

A high fever left Mary blind when she was fourteen, so Laura became her sister's eyes. She described things in detail and repeated her school lessons at night so Mary could learn, too. This early practice must have helped Laura when she became a teacher at fifteen, and later, a writer.

There Laura met her husband, Almanzo Wilder. With their daughter, Rose, they moved to a farm in the Ozark Mountains. It was Laura's last move in a covered wagon. She traveled to many other places, but from then on, she always called Rocky Ridge Farm home.

Laura's daughter, Rose, became an author. When Laura decided to write stories based on her life, she turned to Rose for help. *Little House in the Big Woods*, published in 1932, was so popular that Laura went on to write many more novels about her life as a pioneer girl.

HELEN KELLER

FACT FILE

★ **BORN:** June 27, 1880, in Tuscumbia, Alabama

★ **SPOUSE:** Never Married

★ **CHILDREN:** None

★ **DIED:** June 1, 1968, in Westport, Connecticut

When Helen Keller was just nineteen months old, she had a high fever that left her blind, deaf, and unable to speak. She knew she was different from other people and often became so angry that she kicked and screamed. The inventor Alexander Graham Bell examined her when she was six and arranged for the Perkins Institution for the Blind to send her a teacher.

That teacher, Anne Sullivan, spent hours every day trying to teach Helen the alphabet by spelling letters and words into her hand. One day, Helen suddenly understood the word water. From then on, she was determined to learn everything she could.

With Anne's help, Helen learned to read and write. When she was ten, Helen heard about a deaf and blind child who had learned to speak, and she wanted to speak, too. Anne took her to a teacher in Boston, and soon Helen was able to speak not just in English but in French and German, too.

MIRACLE WORKER

Helen's teacher, Anne Sullivan, was a student at the Perkins Institution and nearly blind herself until two operations restored her vision. She was Helen's teacher and friend from March 1887 until her death in 1936. A play about her early days with Helen, *The Miracle Worker*, was also made into a popular movie.

HUMANITARIAN

PRESIDENTIAL MEETINGS

Helen Keller met President Grover Cleveland when she was only seven years old. She went on to meet the next eleven presidents. The last was President John F. Kennedy in 1961.

Helen wanted to keep learning as much as possible, and that meant going to college. Many people said it wasn't possible for a blind and deaf woman to succeed, but Helen was determined to prove them wrong. She studied hard and was accepted at Radcliffe College. Anne went with her and used the manual alphabet to share all the lectures with Helen. She also read books to her that weren't available in Braille. In 1904, Helen graduated with honors.

She went on to become a bestselling author and traveled around the globe. She even met with presidents and other leaders. Helen forever changed the way the world thought about people with disabilities.

SMELL AND TOUCH

Helen used her senses of smell and touch to substitute for sight and hearing. She could tell, by smell, when she was passing particular buildings, when it was raining, or when the grass was being cut. In addition to the manual alphabet, she could also read lips by placing her fingertips on the mouth of the speaker.

ELEANOR ROOSEVELT

FACT FILE

★ **BORN:** October 11, 1884, in New York, New York
★ **SPOUSE:** Franklin Delano Roosevelt
★ **CHILDREN:** Anna, James, Franklin Jr. (the first, died in infancy), Elliott, Franklin Jr. (the second), John
★ **DIED:** November 7, 1962, in New York, New York

Eleanor Roosevelt's mother thought Eleanor was plain and nicknamed her "Granny." As a young girl, Eleanor was shy and often sad. She became even sadder when both of her parents died by the time she was ten. She then went to live with her strict grandmother.

When she was fifteen, Eleanor's grandmother sent her to school in England. Eleanor's teachers encouraged her to read books and to think for herself. Three years later a more confident girl returned to New York. She taught classes to the poor in the slums, the poorest neighborhoods.

A distant relative, Franklin Delano Roosevelt, wanted to get to know Eleanor better. After a year of meetings and secret letters, he asked her to marry him, and she said yes.

Franklin was elected to the New York State Senate and later took a job in Washington, D.C. Eleanor got involved in politics, too. When Franklin came down with polio, a disease that caused people to become paralyzed, Eleanor acted as her husband's "legs and ears" since he could no longer walk.

UNCLE TEDDY

Eleanor's favorite uncle walked her down the aisle on her wedding day in 1905. He just happened to be the president of the United States, Theodore Roosevelt!

FIRST LADY, CHAMPION OF HUMAN RIGHTS

DAUGHTERS OF THE AMERICAN REVOLUTION

Eleanor was a member of a patriotic group called the Daughters of the American Revolution (DAR)—that is, until they wouldn't let Marian Anderson, a famous singer, perform for them, because she was African American (see "More Amazing Women Who Changed the World" on p. 94). The First Lady quit the organization and arranged for Marian to give her concert on the steps of the Lincoln Memorial in Washington, D.C. On April 9, 1939, seventy-five thousand people of all races came to hear her sing.

When Franklin was elected president in 1932, First Ladies were supposed to be their husband's silent partners. Eleanor took a more public role by giving lectures and writing a newspaper column. She championed the rights of the poor, black people, and women and helped her husband lead the country out of the Great Depression. During World War II, she traveled around the globe bringing hope to the soldiers.

After Franklin's death, President Harry S. Truman appointed Eleanor to the United Nations, where she fought for the rights of people all over the world.

GEORGIA O'KEEFFE

FACT FILE

★ **BORN:** November 15, 1887, near Sun Prairie, Wisconsin

★ **SPOUSE:** Alfred Stieglitz

★ **CHILDREN:** None

★ **DIED:** March 6, 1986, in Santa Fe, New Mexico

Georgia O'Keeffe, who grew up on a farm in Wisconsin, always liked making art. By the time she graduated from high school, Georgia knew she wanted to be an artist.

She studied in Chicago and New York, but the formal rules in art school made her question her early goals. Then she took a class in South Carolina and learned about the less structured and more imaginative world of abstract art. Soon, Georgia developed a style all her own.

Georgia sent drawings in this new style to the world-famous photographer Alfred Stieglitz, and then had her first one-woman show in New York City. Stieglitz, who later became her husband, offered Georgia enough money to quit her teaching job and spend a whole year focusing on her art.

She became famous for her paintings of dramatic skyscrapers and giant flowers. Georgia was soon recognized as one of the country's best new artists.

PRESIDENTIAL MEDALS

In 1977, President Gerald Ford recognized Georgia's contribution to American culture with the Presidential Medal of Freedom, the highest civilian honor in the United States. President Ronald Reagan gave her the National Medal of Arts in 1985.

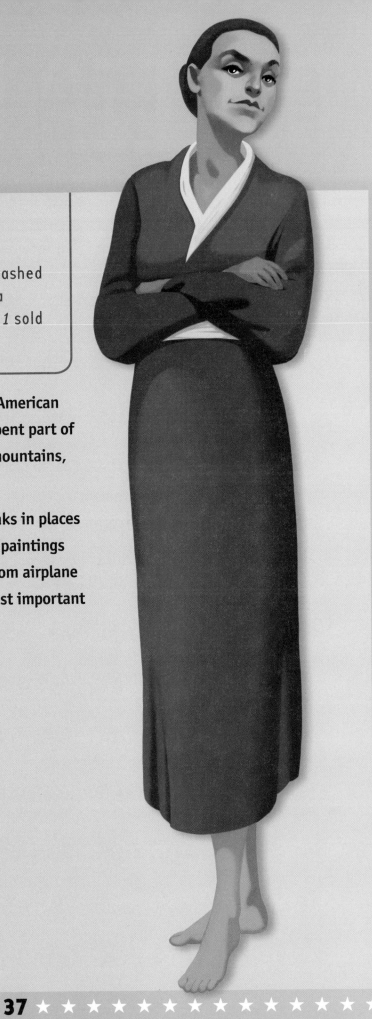

RECORD-BREAKING SALE

In 2014, one of Georgia's flower paintings smashed the previous record for the sale of a work by a female artist. *Jimson Weed, White Flower No. 1* sold for $44 million!

Her work changed in 1929 when she visited the American Southwest. For the next twenty years, Georgia spent part of every year in New Mexico, painting the desert, mountains, and flowers of the Southwest.

In her later years, Georgia painted mountain peaks in places like Japan and Peru. She also created a series of paintings based on the rivers, clouds, and skies she saw from airplane windows. Today, she is considered one of the most important artists of the twentieth century.

AMELIA EARHART

Amelia Earhart, the world's most famous female pilot, always loved adventure. Along with playing sports like basketball and tennis, she loved sledding down icy hills. She and her sister, Muriel, made up a game when they were young that involved using handmade maps to "travel" to imaginary places.

In 1920, Amelia talked her father into paying ten dollars so she could ride in a plane at an air show. When she landed, Amelia announced that she was going to take flying lessons. She worked odd jobs to pay for the lessons herself, and later saved enough to buy her first plane.

In 1928, Amelia was chosen by her future husband to be the first female passenger on a **transatlantic** flight. At the time, air travel—especially across an ocean—was considered very dangerous. Amelia became a sensation. She went on to break many flying records as a pilot, including becoming the first woman to fly alone across the Atlantic Ocean.

DARING ADVENTURES

After a family vacation to the St. Louis World's Fair, Amelia, Muriel, and some friends built a roller coaster in their backyard. Amelia went zooming off the tracks on her very first ride and told her sister it was "just like flying!"

AVIATOR

NURSE'S AIDE

Amelia visited her sister in Canada during World War I. Seeing wounded soldiers, she decided to take a Red Cross first-aid course. With that training, she became a nurse's aide at a military hospital.

Amelia's biggest dream was to be the first pilot to **circumnavigate** the globe at (or as close as possible to) the equator. In June 1937, she set out with her navigator, Fred Noonan. On July 2, after traveling about two-thirds around the globe—over 22,000 miles—Amelia and her plane mysteriously vanished.

Rescue searchers looked for her, Fred, and their plane on land, sea, and air. But no trace of them was ever found. Many people believe they must have crashed into the ocean, but others continue to search for signs of Amelia and her airplane on small Pacific islands.

MARGARET MEAD

TRAILBLAZING ANTHROPOLOGIST

FACT FILE

★ **BORN:** December 16, 1901, in Philadelphia, Pennsylvania

★ **SPOUSE:** Luther Cressman (1923–1928), Reo Fortune (1928–1935),
   Gregory Bateson (1936–1950)

★ **CHILDREN:** Mary Catherine Bateson

★ **DIED:** November 15, 1978, in New York, New York

Margaret Mead grew up in a busy household with her parents, grandmother, and four siblings. Her grandmother thought it was unhealthy to spend too much time indoors, so Margaret spent a lot of time outside, exploring the natural world. At a very young age, she learned to observe and take notes about what was going on around her.

That skill served her well when she decided to study anthropology, a subject that focuses on human beings and their culture. She traveled to the South Pacific to do research for her Ph.D. and wrote a book about what she learned. Her book, *Coming of Age in Samoa*, became a bestseller.

Margaret studied human behavior and how culture is passed down to children. She wrote about the different ways boys and girls are treated in different cultures and how that shapes their society. Her work, which showed Americans what other cultures are like, helped make the big world feel like a smaller place.

CHANGING THE WORLD

Margaret believed that people could work together to end things like racism and war. Her motto was, "Never doubt that a small group of thoughtful, committed citizens can change the world."

MARGARET BOURKE-WHITE

PIONEERING PHOTOJOURNALIST

FACT FILE

★ **BORN:** June 14, 1904, in the Bronx, New York

★ **SPOUSE:** Everett Chapman (1924–1926),
Erskine Caldwell (1939–1942)

★ **CHILDREN:** None

★ **DIED:** August 27, 1971, in Stamford, Connecticut

Margaret White's father was an engineer and an inventor. Her mother taught her that self-improvement was important. Both parents inspired her to pursue her own path in life.

After she graduated from college, Margaret took up photography as a hobby. It wasn't long before she was selling her dramatic photos to newspapers and magazines. She combined her own last name with her mother's maiden name to become Margaret Bourke-White.

Margaret went on assignments all over the world and became famous for her photographs of the Great Depression, modern industry, World War II, and many other subjects. During World War II, she was the first woman ever to work directly with the U.S. Armed Forces to take photographs. She went on bombing runs, was torpedoed on a ship, and was among the first to show the world the horrors of Germany's concentration camps.

After the war, Margaret continued to travel the globe, photographing important world events and natural disasters.

MAGGIE THE INDESTRUCTIBLE

Margaret often took on dangerous assignments. She went on bombing runs over Nazi Germany, became stranded in the Arctic, and survived a helicopter crash. But she always returned alive and well, earning her the nickname "Maggie the Indestructible."

RACHEL CARSON

FACT FILE

★ **BORN:** May 27, 1907, in Springdale, Pennsylvania

★ **SPOUSE:** Never married

★ **CHILDREN:** Roger, adopted in 1956

★ **DIED:** April 14, 1964, in Silver Spring, Maryland

Rachel Carson grew up on a farm and spent most of her time outdoors. She loved to read and write and planned to study English in college, but a biology course changed her mind. So she became a marine biologist, a scientist who studies ocean life.

Rachel's life was dedicated to exploring the ocean. In her free time she wrote stories about the sea, and her books became bestsellers. One scientific trip took her on a ten-day voyage to the area around Nova Scotia, Canada. Two years later, Rachel published *The Sea Around Us*. Her poetic writing style helped teach people about the wonders of the natural world in a new way.

During the 1950s, Rachel became concerned about pesticides, or insect-killing chemicals, that were being used on farms and in gardens. She discovered that they were hurting the environment and wondered what that would mean for birds, animals, and humans.

Rachel did research that proved the pesticides were in our water, air, and soil and were making all sorts of creatures sick—including humans. After six years of study, she published *Silent Spring* in 1962.

EARLY SUCCESS

Rachel started writing poetry when she was eight. Her first story, "A Battle in the Clouds," was published in *St. Nicholas* magazine when she was ten.

ENVIRONMENTALIST

ENVIRONMENTAL PROTECTION AGENCY

When *Silent Spring* was published, President John F. Kennedy called for a special committee of scientists to investigate Rachel's warnings. His committee agreed with Rachel, and Congress passed laws to ban dangerous pesticides. In 1970, they established the Environmental Protection Agency (EPA) to help reduce pollution.

Silent Spring sparked a revolution. Chemical companies called Rachel "hysterical" and said her claims were based on bad science. But people were not fooled. Because of Rachel's research, many dangerous chemicals were banned.

Rachel showed the world that if people continued to destroy nature, we would also destroy ourselves.

BABE DIDRIKSON ZAHARIAS

FACT FILE

★ **BORN:** June 11, 1911, in Port Arthur, Texas

★ **SPOUSE:** George Zaharias

★ **CHILDREN:** None

★ **DIED:** September 27, 1956, in Galveston, Texas

Babe Didrikson Zaharias is considered the greatest female athlete of the twentieth century. Mildred "Babe" Didrikson participated in every sport available at her school. She set records in track and field, was an All-American in basketball, a great tennis player, and a star on the baseball team. But that wasn't enough. When Babe wasn't playing team sports, she was working on her golf game, or diving, roller-skating, cycling, or bowling.

She made the women's track-and-field team for the 1932 Olympics in Los Angeles and came home with three medals. The world began to call her "Wonder Girl."

Eventually, Babe realized she was going to have to focus on one sport, and she chose golf. She was paired with wrestler George Zaharias at a 1938 golf tournament, and married him by the end of the year. The couple traveled all over the world so Babe could play golf. She not only won almost every tournament she entered, she also made golf a popular sport for women.

BABE

Neighborhood boys are said to have given Babe her nickname when she hit five home runs in one baseball game, just like New York Yankee Babe Ruth.

OLYMPIC MEDALS

Babe read about the 1928 Olympics in the newspaper and decided she'd compete in track and field in 1932. She and her sister practiced by jumping over hedges. Babe qualified for five events on the 1932 team, but women were only allowed to enter three. She set world records and won two gold medals and one silver in hurdles, javelin, and the high jump.

Babe was still winning tournaments when she was diagnosed with colon cancer in 1953. Back then, many people didn't talk openly about cancer, but Babe did. She wanted to help others by making them aware of the symptoms. She died three years later.

LUCILLE BALL

FACT FILE

★ **BORN:** August 6, 1911, in Celeron, near Jamestown, New York

★ **SPOUSE:** Desi Arnaz (1940–1960), Gary Morton (1961–1989)

★ **CHILDREN:** Lucie, Desi Jr.

★ **DIED:** April 26, 1989, in Los Angeles, California

Lucille Ball's favorite childhood memories involved going to shows and silent movies and putting on plays. When she was fifteen, she went to New York City to study acting.

In New York, Lucy was told that she didn't have any talent. She went home, but didn't give up. Two years later, she returned to Manhattan, and this time she started getting small parts.

One part led to another, and Lucy worked with many great comedians like the Marx Brothers and the Three Stooges. She dyed her hair bright red for one part, and that became her signature look.

Lucy met Cuban bandleader Desi Arnaz on a film set and married him in 1940. The couple wanted to find a way to work together, so they wrote a pilot for a TV show about a wacky woman who was married to a Cuban bandleader. TV studios weren't interested, so they took their act on the road, performing around the country. Finally, they set up their own TV production company to make the show themselves.

QUEEN OF THE B MOVIES

"B" movies were low-budget films that were shown in theaters as part of a double feature with bigger, more popular movies. Lucy made more than forty-three "B" films in the 1930s and became know as the "Queen of the B Movies."

COMEDIAN

GET THAT GIRL'S NAME

Lucy played one of twelve girls in the film *Roman Scandals*. She even volunteered to be the one girl hit in the face with a pie. The director reportedly said, "Get that girl's name. That's the one who will make it [in Hollywood]."

I Love Lucy first aired on October 15, 1951, and was a huge hit. Lucy became the most famous face on television, but she was more than just a funny actress who made people laugh. Lucy was the president of her own production company! After her divorce from Desi, she made more "Lucy" shows. Lucy had created a character that her fans didn't want to live without.

EVERYONE LOVES LUCY

You can still catch *I Love Lucy* reruns on television stations all over the world. It is the longest-running program in Los Angeles, almost sixty years after Lucy, Desi, and the rest of the gang stopped making shows.

JULIA CHILD

FACT FILE

★ **BORN:** August 15, 1912, in Pasadena, California

★ **SPOUSE:** Paul Child

★ **CHILDREN:** None

★ **DIED:** August 13, 2004, in Montecito, California

The most famous American chef, Julia Child, didn't grow up cooking. She loved sports, maybe because she was stronger and taller than other girls her age. She eventually grew to be six feet two. After college, Julia decided she wanted to be a writer.

When World War II broke out, Julia joined the Office of Strategic Services (OSS), which later became the CIA. She was sent to the island country now known as Sri Lanka, and later to China. One of her fellow OSS members, Paul Child, loved gourmet food. He and Julia often had dinner together, sampling the local foods.

After the war, they decided to get married. Julia wanted to take a cooking course, but she was terrible at it. When Paul, a diplomat, was posted to Paris, Julia got serious about learning to cook. She studied at the famous Le Cordon Bleu cooking school. Soon, Julia was making delicious meals.

BON APPÉTIT!

Julia always ended her television show with the words "Bon appétit!," French for "Good appetite," or "Enjoy your meal!"

Two French friends asked Julia for help in writing a French cookbook for Americans. It took many years, but *Mastering the Art of French Cooking* was published in 1961. It sold more than 100,000 copies in one year— a number that was unheard of for a cookbook.

JULIA'S KITCHEN

By the time Julia and Paul moved to their house in Cambridge, Massachusetts, Julia had cooked in eight different homes. She knew exactly how she wanted to arrange her new kitchen in Cambridge, and she cooked there for forty years. When the Smithsonian Institution learned Julia was moving to California in 2001, they asked for her kitchen! Today, you can visit Julia's kitchen, on display in Washington, D.C.

Julia was interviewed about the book on a Boston television station. She brought a bowl, a whisk, and some eggs to make the interview more entertaining. Before long she had her own cooking show! *The French Chef* was an instant success. People liked her enthusiasm and the fact that she sometimes made mistakes. Julia spent the rest of her life making meals on TV, showing Americans that cooking can be both fun and delicious.

ROSA PARKS

FACT FILE

★ **BORN:** February 4, 1913, in Tuskegee, Alabama
★ **SPOUSE:** Raymond Parks
★ **CHILDREN:** None
★ **DIED:** October 24, 2005, in Detroit, Michigan

Rosa McCauley, her mother, and her younger brother moved to her grandparents' farm when she was two years old, after her father left the family. There were no public schools for black children in rural Alabama, so Rosa attended a school run by a local church. When she was eleven, she went to live with an aunt in Montgomery so that she could continue her schooling. She cleaned classrooms to help pay her tuition.

In 1932, Rosa married Raymond Parks. He was a member of the National Association for the Advancement of Colored People (NAACP). Rosa was one of the first women to join the Montgomery chapter of the organization.

In 1950s Alabama, only white people were allowed to sit in the front of the public buses. If the white section was full, black people in the "colored" section had to stand so that whites could sit. On December 1, 1955, Rosa was sitting in the bus's colored section when a white man told her to move. Rosa said no and was arrested.

SEGREGATION

The South had many laws, known as Jim Crow laws, that kept white and black people apart. Black people couldn't vote, couldn't hold good jobs, and couldn't eat in the same restaurants as white people. They had separate bathrooms and drinking fountains. Black schools weren't as good as white schools. In 1964, Congress passed the Civil Rights Act, which finally banned segregation (or keeping people separate) as illegal and unjust.

CIVIL RIGHTS ACTIVIST

A LIGHT IN THE DARKNESS

The nation of Sweden celebrated Rosa Parks, calling her "a light in the darkness" and creating the Rosa Parks Peace Prize in her honor. Rosa received awards from all over the world, including the Presidential Medal of Freedom and the Congressional Gold Medal. In 2013, a statue of Rosa Parks was unveiled in the United States Capitol.

Her refusal sparked the NAACP to call for a bus **boycott**. Blacks refused to ride the buses. Since most bus riders were black, the bus company suffered, but they still wouldn't change their rules. Then, on June 19, 1956, a federal court ruled that bus segregation was **unconstitutional**. The Supreme Court agreed, and the city of Montgomery was forced to change the bus rules. The boycott had lasted 381 days.

Rosa inspired others to protest unfair laws. But because of her actions, which many people still did not agree with, she and her husband lost their jobs and even received death threats. In 1957, they moved to Detroit, Michigan, where Rosa continued to fight for civil rights for the rest of her life.

BARBARA McCLINTOCK

GENETICIST

FACT FILE

★ **BORN:** June 16, 1902, in Hartford, Connecticut

★ **SPOUSE:** Never married

★ **CHILDREN:** None

★ **DIED:** September 2, 1992, in Huntington, New York

Barbara McClintock loved nature, even after her family moved from Connecticut to Brooklyn, New York. Her father was a doctor, and Barbara had an interest in science, too. When it was time to go to college, she decided to study biology at Cornell University. Girls were not allowed to major in genetics (the study of genes, which are transferred from parents to children and determine things like what color eyes you will have), so Barbara studied botany to earn her Ph.D. She also took genetics courses and began to study the genetics of corn. She wanted to know why some kernels of Indian corn have a mixture of colors and others don't.

After college, Barbara had a hard time finding a university or research lab that would hire a woman, but she didn't give up. She was eventually hired by a lab where she discovered that chromosomes, which carry genes, can move or "jump" from one place to another on DNA.

At first Barbara's work was ignored, but then other scientists realized how important it was. In 1983, she became the first woman to be the sole winner of the Nobel Prize for Medicine.

SMITHSONIAN

After her death, Barbara's favorite microscope was donated to the Smithsonian Institution in Washington, D.C., in the hope that it would inspire more young people, and especially girls, to study science.

GERTRUDE ELION

PHARMACOLOGIST

Gertrude Elion grew up in the Bronx (northern New York City), where she loved to visit the Bronx Zoo. She also loved school and learning and had a hard time settling on just one thing to study in college. Then she thought of her grandfather, who died of cancer when she was fifteen, and realized that she wanted to help find a cure. She decided to major in chemistry. When the man she was going to marry died when she was twenty-three, Gertrude became more determined than ever to cure diseases.

It was almost impossible back then for a female chemist to find work. Gertrude accepted jobs at whatever labs would take her, sometimes for no money. Finally, she was hired by a lab that allowed her to do the research she loved—discovering new medicines to treat diseases. She and her research partner, George Hitchings, came up with new and better ways to develop drugs.

In 1988, Gertrude and George, along with James Whyte Black, received the Nobel Prize for Medicine for their lifesaving scientific work.

LIFESAVER

Gertrude and her research partner developed medicines that treat childhood leukemia and allow kidney patients to receive transplants, along with many other drugs. More than a million people are alive today because of Gertrude's work!

ELLA FITZGERALD

FACT FILE

★ **BORN:** April 25, 1918, in Newport News, Virginia
★ **SPOUSE:** Bernie Kornegay (1941–1943),
  Ray Brown (1948–1952)
★ **CHILDREN:** Raymond, Jr. (adopted)
★ **DIED:** June 15, 1996, in Beverly Hills, California

Ella Fitzgerald, known as "the First Lady of Song," was born in Virginia. Her parents separated when she was one, and she moved to Yonkers, New York, with her mother. Ella and her younger sister, Frances, loved to dance. They would dance around their apartment while their mother sang along to records. Ella also joined the glee club at school.

In her early teens, Ella discovered the bustling African American neighborhood of Harlem, which was just a trolley car and a subway ride away. She went to the Savoy Ballroom and learned the latest dances, bringing them back to Yonkers and dancing on street corners for spare change.

Ella was sixteen, tall, and shy when her friends dared her to enter a talent contest at Harlem's famous Apollo Theater. She planned to dance, but Ella was so nervous when she hit the stage that she couldn't move her feet. She had to do something, so she sang instead. Her voice was shaky at first, but it grew stronger. Ella ended up winning first prize!

SCAT AND BEBOP

Ella made scat singing popular, which is singing nonsense syllables like "skee-ba-doobie-do-wah" to imitate musical instruments. It went along with a new kind of jazz music—bebop.

JAZZ SINGER

JAIL TIME

When Ella went on tour, her manager insisted that she and the other black musicians be treated the same as whites, even when they traveled in the South. Once in Texas the police went backstage to give the black performers a hard time. When they saw band members gambling in Ella's dressing room, they arrested everyone, including Ella. Then they had the nerve to ask Ella for an autograph in jail!

She kept winning talent shows, and soon she was the lead singer for a jazz band performing at the Savoy Ballroom. Ella was a hit! Her fans especially loved it when she left the stage and danced with the audience. She sang with lots of famous bands and recorded many albums.

Among her numerous honors are thirteen Grammy awards, over 40 million albums sold, and the National Medal of Arts given to her by President Ronald Reagan.

NANCY REAGAN

FACT FILE

★ **BORN:** July 6, 1921, in Queens, New York

★ **SPOUSE:** Ronald Reagan

★ **CHILDREN:** Patricia Ann, Ronald Prescott

        Stepchildren: Maureen Elizabeth, Michael Edward

★ **DIED:** March 6, 2016, in Los Angeles, California

Anne Frances Robbins, nicknamed "Nancy," was born in New York City. Her parents separated soon after she was born, and Nancy's mother sent her to live with relatives while she worked as an actress. Living apart from her mother was hard for Nancy. When her mother remarried in 1929, Nancy was able to live with her again, and she was adopted by her stepfather.

In school, Nancy joined student government and acted in class plays. She majored in theater at Smith College. After graduation she performed on Broadway and then moved to Hollywood to make movies.

In Hollywood, Nancy met and married an actor named Ronald Reagan. When her husband entered politics, Nancy was at his side on the campaign trail, and he was elected governor of California. As First Lady of the state, Nancy worked hard to make sure that wounded Vietnam War veterans had the money they needed. She also raised funds for the families of soldiers who were prisoners of war or missing in action.

MOVIE MAGIC

Nancy performed in eleven films from 1949 to 1956. Her first role was in *Shadow on the Wall*. She and Ronald Reagan starred opposite each other in her last movie, *Hellcats of the Navy*.

FIRST LADY, ANTI-DRUG ACTIVIST

FOSTER GRANDPARENTS

Nancy started the "Foster Grandparents Program" in California to bring together senior citizens and young people. It has since spread to the rest of the country.

When her husband was elected president, Nancy was again at his side. She helped him choose key staff members and guarded both his time and his health. She raised private funds to redecorate the White House, something that was long overdue. Nancy also took on the issue of drug and alcohol abuse by teenagers. She spoke at schools and events all over the country to encourage young people to stay away from drugs and alcohol with the words "Just Say No!"

After her husband's death from Alzheimer's, Nancy worked to raise money for research into preventing and curing this disease.

MARIA TALLCHIEF

Elizabeth Marie "Maria" Tall Chief was born on an Osage
Indian reservation in Oklahoma. Her father was Osage, and
her mother was descended from Scots-Irish pioneers. Maria and her
sister, Marjorie, played the piano and danced. Their mother saw how talented the girls were,
and didn't think they would get the education they needed in Oklahoma. When Maria was
eight, the family moved to California. The first thing they went to see was the ocean.

In California, Maria studied with a number of music and dance teachers. When she was twelve,
her father told her she had to choose ballet or piano, and she chose to focus on ballet. When
she was seventeen she traveled to New York City to see the Ballet Russe. The company soon
asked Maria to join them. One of their choreographers, George Balanchine, began to create
dances for Maria, and even asked her to marry him.

NATIVE AMERICAN CUSTOMS

When Maria was little, Native Americans were often discriminated against. Federal
and state governments ruled that Osage language and culture were against the law.
The Osage people performed their forbidden dances, spoke their language, and held
their religious ceremonies in secret.

BALLERINA

WHAT'S IN A NAME?

In California, Maria was teased about her Native American heritage. Her two-word last name confused people. Many ballerinas were Russian, and friends suggested she change her name to Tallchieva to sound Russian. But Maria was proud of her heritage. To make things easier, she combined Tall Chief into one name and performed as Maria Tallchief.

When Balanchine started a brand-new dance company, the New York City Ballet, he created more roles just for Maria. In 1949, she performed in *Firebird*, the ballet that made her famous. She dazzled audiences with her speed, grace, and energy.

Maria danced with the NYCB until 1965. When she retired she opened a dance school in Chicago, passing down her knowledge and love of dance to the next generation of ballerinas.

BARBARA BUSH

FACT FILE

★ **BORN:** June 8, 1925, in New York, New York

★ **SPOUSE:** George H. W. Bush

★ **CHILDREN:** George W., Pauline (Robin), John (Jeb),

Neil, Marvin, Dorothy

★ **DIED:** Still alive

Barbara Pierce had a happy childhood growing up in the suburbs of New York City. Her family inspired her to love reading. She also liked to swim and ride her bicycle. In college, she became captain of the freshman soccer team.

She met George H. W. Bush at a Christmas dance when she was sixteen. Their high schools were far apart, but they wrote each other letters. A year and a half later they became engaged just before George entered World War II as a navy pilot. Barbara worked at a factory to help the war effort. When George came home on leave, they got married.

After the war, George finished college and they moved to Texas to start their lives together. They had six children. Sadly, their daughter Robin died of leukemia when she was three.

When George was elected vice president in 1980, Barbara took up the cause of literacy. She believed that if more people could read and write, it would help reduce poverty, drug abuse, disease, and homelessness. Barbara continued to advocate for literacy when George became president in 1989. She also encouraged Americans to volunteer their time to make the world a better place.

FIRST MOM

Barbara Bush and Abigail Adams belong to a very small club. They are the only two women who were both a wife *and* a mother of an American president.

FIRST LADY, LITERACY ADVOCATE

AUTHOR, AUTHOR!

While in the White House, Barbara wrote two books: *C. Fred's Story*, the tale of a family dog living in Washington, D.C., and *Millie's Book*, the First Dog's view of life in the White House. Barbara donated all of her earnings to literacy causes.

After leaving the White House, Barbara helped her sons Jeb and George W. in their campaigns to be the governors of Florida and Texas, and in George W.'s successful run for president in 2000.

FIRST HUSBAND?

Barbara knows women can do anything that men can do. She once spoke to a group of Wellesley College graduates and got a huge round of applause when she said, "Who knows? Somewhere out in this audience may even be someone who will one day follow in my footsteps and preside over the White House as the president's spouse. And I wish *him* well."

CORETTA SCOTT KING

FACT FILE

★ **BORN:** April 27, 1927, in Heiberger, Alabama

★ **SPOUSE:** Martin Luther King, Jr.

★ **CHILDREN:** Yolanda, Martin Luther III, Dexter, Bernice

★ **DIED:** January 30, 2006, in Rosarito, Mexico

Coretta Scott grew up on a small farm. She and her two siblings helped out by feeding the chickens and pigs, milking cows, and tending the garden. She also worked picking cotton.

Coretta walked six miles to and from school every day while white children rode buses to better schools. Her parents worked hard to send her to a private high school, where she became interested in music.

Coretta won a scholarship to study music and education at a college in Ohio, but discovered racism there, too. When it was time for her to be a student teacher, the public school refused to allow her to teach because she was black. That only made Coretta more determined than ever to fight for civil rights.

She was studying music in Boston when she met a young minister named Martin Luther King, Jr. She married him in 1953, and they moved to Montgomery, Alabama. Martin quickly became a leader in the civil rights movement, and Coretta planned marches and boycotts. She gave concerts and speeches all over the country.

OBEY?

When Coretta married Martin, most brides promised to "love, honor, and obey" their husbands. Coretta made it clear before her wedding that she would not promise to obey. Martin's father, a minister, was shocked, but he agreed to leave the word out of their wedding vows.

CIVIL RIGHTS ACTIVIST

MARTIN LUTHER KING, JR. DAY

Coretta thought her husband's birthday should be remembered, and she worked hard to make it a national holiday. In 1983, President Ronald Reagan signed a bill making the third Monday in January Martin Luther King, Jr. Day.

After Martin was **assassinated** in 1968, Coretta continued to lead the effort for civil rights. Four days after his murder, she and three of her children led the march that Martin had organized. She also founded the Martin Luther King, Jr. Center for Nonviolent Social Change (now called the King Center) in Atlanta.

BOOK AWARDS

Literacy was important to Coretta, and she wanted black authors and illustrators to be celebrated. The Coretta Scott King Book Awards are given every year to outstanding African American authors and illustrators of books for children and young adults.

PATSY TAKEMOTO MINK

FACT FILE

★ **BORN:** December 6, 1927, in Paia, Hawaii

★ **SPOUSE:** John Mink

★ **CHILDREN:** Gwendolyn

★ **DIED:** September 28, 2002, in Honolulu, Hawaii

Patsy Takemoto grew up in Hawaii, where she was president and valedictorian of her high school class. She planned to go to medical school, but she couldn't find one that would accept a woman. She went to law school instead, but discovered that law firms didn't hire women. So she started her own law firm in Hawaii.

She also became involved in local politics. When Hawaii, a territory, was made a U.S. state in 1959, Patsy ran for Congress. She lost her first race, but she didn't give up. In 1964, she became the first non-white woman to be elected to the House of Representatives.

Patsy won reelection many times and served in Congress until 1977. She concentrated on issues such as health care, education, women's rights, and protecting the environment. She also supported President Lyndon Johnson's programs to help the poor and promote civil rights.

PEARL HARBOR

Patsy was fourteen when Japanese planes bombed Pearl Harbor, Hawaii, in December 1941 and the United States entered World War II. Patsy's Japanese-American family had lived on Maui for three generations, but her father was taken away and questioned. He returned home the next day, but the family lived in fear until the end of the war.

CONGRESSWOMAN

TITLE IX

Patsy is best known for writing and helping to pass Title IX of the Education Amendments of 1972. Title IX made gender discrimination in academics and athletics illegal at schools receiving money from the federal government. The law changed the country— girls were now able to study at the same schools and participate in the same sports as boys.

In 1977, Patsy left Congress but remained active in politics and in environmental issues. In 1990, she was elected to the House of Representatives again and remained in Congress for the rest of her life.

On November 24, 2014, after her death, she was awarded the Presidential Medal of Freedom by President Barack Obama.

MAYA ANGELOU

FACT FILE

★ **BORN:** April 4, 1928, in St. Louis, Missouri

★ **SPOUSE:** Tosh Angelos (1951–1954),
Paul Du Feu (1973–1981)

★ **CHILDREN:** Guy Johnson

★ **DIED:** May 28, 2014, in Winston-Salem, North Carolina

Maya Angelou was born Marguerite Johnson. After her parents divorced when she was three, she was raised by her grandmother "Momma" Henderson in Stamps, Arkansas. Life for a poor black girl was difficult in the South. Maya's life was even harder because she was abused by one of her mother's boyfriends. After she told her family and the man was punished, Maya stopped speaking. She didn't say a word for five years, but she grew to love language and the sound of words. She became an excellent listener.

Maya left high school, gave birth to her son, and became the first female streetcar conductor in San Francisco. She also studied dance and music and had a career on the stage. Later she got involved in the civil rights movement and worked with both Martin Luther King, Jr., and Malcolm X.

PRESIDENTIAL POETRY

Maya wrote a poem to read at President Bill Clinton's inauguration in 1993. Her reading of "On the Pulse of Morning" was heard all over the world. In 2005, she wrote "Amazing Peace" for President George W. Bush and read it at the White House's Christmas tree lighting ceremony. President Barack Obama presented Maya with the Presidential Medal of Freedom, the country's highest civilian honor, in 2010.

★ AUTHOR

A BRAVE AND STARTLING TRUTH

In December 2014, Maya's poem "A Brave and Startling Truth" was on board NASA's spacecraft *Orion* for its first unmanned test flight. *Orion* will one day carry astronauts deep into the solar system, maybe even to Mars. NASA wanted to include Maya's poem because it is about human ambition and big dreams.

In the 1960s, Maya was encouraged to become a writer. She took the name Maya Angelou and published her first and most famous book, *I Know Why the Caged Bird Sings*, in 1969. It was a huge bestseller. At the same time, Maya worked in film and television and became the first black female director in Hollywood. She also occasionally acted.

Maya went on to write many poems and plays, and six more autobiographical books. She also served on presidential committees for Gerald Ford and Jimmy Carter. Maya became a symbol of peace and equality all over the world.

HARPER LEE

NOVELIST

FACT FILE

★ **BORN:** April 28, 1926, in Monroeville, Alabama
★ **SPOUSE:** Never married
★ **CHILDREN:** None
★ **DIED:** February 19, 2016, in Monroeville, Alabama

Nelle Harper Lee was born in the small Alabama town of Monroeville. She set her famous novel, *To Kill a Mockingbird*, in a similar town called Maycomb and had a childhood that resembled that of her main character, Scout Finch.

Nelle wrote for student publications in college. She went to law school like her father, but left to move to New York City and become a writer. In the early 1950s, she worked for an airline as a reservations clerk and wrote whenever she could.

One Christmas, friends surprised Nelle with enough money to live on for a year so that she could finish her novel. An editor who liked the character of Scout suggested that Nelle rewrite the book from a younger Scout's point of view, which Nelle did.

To Kill a Mockingbird was published in 1960 under the name Harper Lee. The novel became a huge success and was made into a movie. By 2015, it had sold more than 40 million copies worldwide.

Nelle didn't write another novel after that, but in 2015, her original manuscript was discovered. *Go Set a Watchman*, which takes place twenty years after the events of *To Kill a Mockingbird* and features the same beloved characters, was published on July 14, 2015.

BOOK BUDDIES

Nelle and another famous writer, Truman Capote, grew up next door to each other. Nelle based the character Dill on Truman. And Truman based a character in his novel *Other Voices, Other Rooms* on Nelle.

BARBARA WALTERS

JOURNALIST

FACT FILE

★ **BORN:** September 25, 1929, in Boston, Massachusetts

★ **SPOUSE:** Robert Henry Katz (1955–1958), Lee Guber (1963–1976),

Merv Adelson (1981–1984 and 1986–1992)

★ **CHILDREN:** Jacqueline Dena Guber, adopted in 1968

★ **DIED:** Still alive

Barbara Walters's father owned an East Coast chain of nightclubs called the Latin Quarter. The family moved from Boston to Miami to New York as the business expanded, and Barbara grew up surrounded by singers, showgirls, acrobats, and comedians. Perhaps that's why she was so comfortable interviewing everyone from world leaders to celebrities when she became a television journalist.

Barbara found her career almost by accident. After graduating from college, she became a writer for the *Today* show. When they needed a new "Today Girl" to read commercials, Barbara began appearing on the air. Soon, she was contributing much more and became a popular morning TV host.

Ten years later, Barbara moved to ABC and became the first woman ever to co-anchor an evening newscast. She spent many years co-hosting a television news magazine and later created a daytime TV talk show, *The View*, with a panel of women.

Throughout her career, Barbara was known for her interviews with everyone from presidents and world leaders to criminals and celebrities. She retired from *The View* in 2014, but remains one of the greatest TV journalists of all time.

PRESIDENTS AND FIRST LADIES

Barbara has interviewed every president and First Lady from Richard and Pat Nixon through Barack and Michelle Obama.

DIAN FOSSEY

FACT FILE

★ **BORN:** January 16, 1932, in San Francisco, California

★ **SPOUSE:** Never married

★ **CHILDREN:** None

★ **DIED:** December 26, 1985, in Rwanda

Dian Fossey's parents divorced when she was three, and her childhood was sometimes difficult. Her mother remarried, but Dian's stepfather didn't treat her well. She worked hard in school and went to college to be a therapist for disabled children. Dian loved her job, but she wanted to see the world. In 1963, she used her savings and borrowed money from the bank to travel to Africa.

When she got there, Dian met **anthropologist** Louis Leakey, who introduced her to mountain gorillas. Dian was fascinated, but she had to go home and work to repay her loan from the bank. She impressed Leakey so much during her trip that he flew to the United States to convince her to move to Africa and study gorillas.

Dian lived among the gorillas in the Virunga Mountains of Rwanda, one of the last wild gorilla habitats left in the world. Unlike other researchers who just watched the animals, Dian acted like one of them. She got down on her knees and knuckles, munched on the same greens they did, and mimicked the sounds they made. Soon, Dian was able to hug 400-pound apes and play with their children.

HOW DO YOU SPELL THAT?

Rwandans gave Dian the nickname "Nyiramachabelli," which means "the woman who lives alone on the mountain."

ZOOLOGIST

ENDANGERED

Mountain gorillas, which live in forests high in the mountains of Africa, continue to be threatened by poachers and by war. Humans have taken over parts of their territory, and the gorillas have been forced to move higher and higher in the mountains where survival is more difficult. Zoologists thought the gorillas might be extinct by now, but they've managed to survive. In 2015, there were approximately 880 wild mountain gorillas left in the world.

Almost everything we know about gorillas, we know because of Dian's work. She showed us that they are gentle creatures that have families very similar to humans.

Dian often battled with poachers, the hunters who kill gorillas illegally and sell their babies to zoos. On December 27, 1985, she was found in her campsite, murdered. Her killer has never been captured, but he was probably one of those poachers. Dian was buried in a cemetery in Africa that she had created for the gorillas.

GLORIA STEINEM

Gloria Steinem spent her early years traveling around in a trailer with her parents. They divorced in 1946 when Gloria was twelve years old, and she and her mother settled in Toledo. There, she was able to attend school on a regular basis for the first time. Her mother was often depressed, and Gloria had to take care of her.

Gloria graduated from Smith College and went to India for two years, where she learned about nonviolent protest. She returned home to become a journalist. As a freelance writer, Gloria was often given "women's" stories. At the time, women had few legal rights, and high-paying jobs were only available to men. Gloria covered these issues as a journalist. Then, in 1969, she became an **activist**, fighting for equal rights for women. Soon, she was leading the **feminist** movement.

EQUAL RIGHTS AMENDMENT

The Equal Rights Amendment, or ERA, guarantees equal rights and equal pay to women under the law. It has been introduced in every Congress since 1982, but has never passed. Thirty-eight states must vote yes before an amendment is added to the Constitution. Opponents to the ERA believe that women will lose some "women's" rights (women, for instance, cannot be drafted in time of war) if it is passed. People who are in favor of the ERA say it is necessary because federal and state laws still discriminate against women, even today.

FEMINIST

FEMINIST ROOTS

Gloria's grandmother fought for women's right to vote. Her father's mother was president of the Ohio Women's Suffrage Association from 1908 to 1911. Gloria herself helped found a women's political organization—the National Women's Political Caucus—in 1971. The group is still active today.

Gloria testified in the Senate on behalf of the Equal Rights Amendment (see sidebar). She also helped launch *Ms.* in 1972, the first magazine ever to be created, owned, and operated by women. The first issue sold out in less than a week.

After running *Ms.* for fifteen years, Gloria became a bestselling author and activist for women's rights around the world. She continues the fight today. In 2013, she was awarded the Presidential Medal of Freedom in recognition of her life-changing work.

HILLARY RODHAM CLINTON

FACT FILE

★ **BORN:** October 26, 1947, in Chicago, Illinois

★ **SPOUSE:** William "Bill" Jefferson Clinton

★ **CHILDREN:** Chelsea

★ **DIED:** Still alive

Hillary Rodham's mother told her daughter that she could be anything she wanted to be. Hillary took ballet and played tennis, softball, and volleyball. She was active in her church and volunteered as a young girl to raise funds for poor children.

In high school, Hillary was voted class president. At Wellesley College, she joined the effort to bring in more black students. She went on to Yale Law School, where she met her future husband, Bill Clinton.

After graduating, Hillary worked for the Children's Defense Fund in Washington, D.C. When Bill became governor of Arkansas, Hillary continued to promote children's rights, especially in education and health care.

Hillary brought that same focus on children and health care to the White House when Bill was elected president in 1992. She created some controversy by getting more involved in government policy than previous First Ladies, and again when she decided to have her own political career. Hillary was elected senator from New York in 2000, just as her husband's second term as president was ending.

BADGE ENVY

Hillary was both a Brownie and a Girl Scout, and she earned every single badge there was.

POLITICIAN

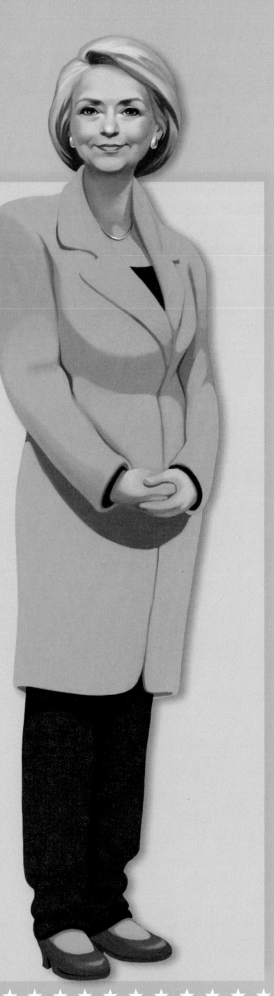

REPUBLICAN TO DEMOCRAT

Most people know Hillary as a member of the Democratic Party, but she started out as a Republican. In high school, she campaigned for Republican candidates, and was president of the Young Republicans Club at Wellesley College her freshman year. Her views about the civil rights movement and the Vietnam War gradually changed, and by the time she left college, Hillary was a Democrat.

In 2007, Hillary declared that she was running for president. By the next June, it was clear that the Democratic Party was going to support Barack Obama, and Hillary dropped out of the race. Then she surprised everyone by agreeing to become President Obama's secretary of state. Hillary spent four years as secretary of state, traveling all over the world. In her first 100 days, she traveled more than 70,000 miles.

In 2015, Hillary announced that she was running for president again. Will she be our first female president of the United States? Only time will tell!

SALLY RIDE

Sally Ride loved the outdoors. Growing up in California, she swam, fished, skied, and skated. Later, she got involved in sports like volleyball and softball, but her favorite was tennis.

Analyzing baseball numbers got Sally hooked on math. She also loved science and had a chemistry set and a telescope when she was young. Math and science came easy to Sally, but she was shy. She hated to be called on in class, even when she knew the answer.

Physics, the study of matter and energy, was the branch of science that interested her the most. She dreamed of becoming an astronaut. She was working on her doctorate degree at Stanford when she saw an ad in the school newspaper inviting women to apply to NASA's astronaut program. Sally applied and was one of six women picked.

WHAT'S OUT THERE?

In high school, Sally and her best friend, Susan Okie, used to watch television shows like *The Twilight Zone* and *Star Trek* on sleepovers and have long discussions about space, wondering, "What's out there?"

Sally worked hard at NASA (the National Aeronautics and Space Administration) and when she blasted into space aboard the *Challenger* on June 18, 1983, she became the first American woman—and, at thirty-two, the youngest American ever—in space. When the shuttle landed, Sally said, "I'm sure it was the most fun that I'll ever have in my life."

★ ASTRONAUT

ASTRONAUT TRAINING

Sally's astronaut training included jumping from airplanes with a parachute, water survival, space navigation, and getting used to zero gravity. She also had to learn to fly a jet plane.

Her next mission on the *Challenger*, in 1984, lasted for eight days. She was training for a third when NASA canceled the program.

Sally left NASA in 1987 to teach at the University of California. She also wrote a number of children's books about Earth, the solar system, and exploring space. She wanted to inspire other girls to pursue science, math, and engineering.

In 2013, after her death, she was awarded the Presidential Medal of Freedom for her groundbreaking achievements.

OPRAH WINFREY

Oprah Winfrey is one of the most powerful women in the world. She probably wouldn't have believed it as a little girl growing up in rural Mississippi. Her parents separated before she was born, and Oprah lived on a farm with her grandparents. By age three she was reciting Sunday school lessons in church, and skipped ahead to first grade soon after she started kindergarten.

When she was nine, Oprah moved to Milwaukee to live with her mother. They were poor, and Oprah was abused by a cousin and other male relatives. By fourteen, she was getting into trouble and went to live with her father in Nashville. He was strict and made sure Oprah did well in school. Soon, she was winning speech contests and working in radio. In college, she got a part-time job as a TV reporter.

Oprah became co-host of a morning show in Baltimore and the number of people watching soared. She moved to Chicago, and the same thing happened there. Soon, she had a talk show named after her that was broadcast nationwide, featuring both celebrities and ordinary people. It became the most successful talk show in television history.

WHAT'S IN A NAME?

Oprah's name was supposed to be Orpah, after a woman in the Bible. It was misspelled Oprah on her birth certificate, and the name stuck.

MEDIA MOGUL

GIVING BACK

Oprah has raised and donated billions of dollars to charities over the years. She is most proud of the Oprah Winfrey Leadership Academy for Girls, a boarding school for gifted girls in South Africa who otherwise could not afford to go to a good school.

Oprah also took on acting roles and was nominated for an Academy Award. She started a television production company and a magazine, produced movies and Broadway musicals, and, as she was bringing her talk show to an end after twenty-five years, founded her own TV network.

Today, Oprah is indeed the "Queen of All Media."

SONIA SOTOMAYOR

FACT FILE

★ **BORN:** June 25, 1954, in New York, New York

★ **SPOUSE:** Kevin Noonan (1976–1983)

★ **CHILDREN:** None

★ **DIED:** Still alive

No one would have believed that a girl from one of the poorest neighborhoods in New York City, the South Bronx, would grow up to be the first Hispanic Supreme Court justice. But that's exactly what Sonia Sotomayor did.

Sonia was the oldest child of Puerto Rican parents who moved to the United States. The family had lots of love, but they struggled with poverty and other hardships. When she was eight, Sonia was diagnosed with a disease called diabetes. She has to give herself shots of insulin to stay healthy. When she was nine, Sonia's father died.

Her mother worked hard to send Sonia and her brother, Juan, to good schools. Sonia studied a lot and graduated from high school at the top of her class. She received scholarships to Princeton University and later, Yale Law School.

GIRL DETECTIVE

When she finished her homework, Sonia loved to read Nancy Drew novels. Her first dream was to become a detective. After she was diagnosed with diabetes, she decided another job might be better. She saw a TV show about lawyers and judges and decided that would be her new dream.

SUPREME COURT JUSTICE

PLAY BALL!

When Sonia, a Yankee fan, was a district court judge, she ended a Major League Baseball strike that would have ruined the 1995 baseball season. Many fans believe that she saved baseball!

Sonia worked as a lawyer for many years, and in 1992, President George H. W. Bush nominated her for a judgeship on the U.S. District Court. She was the first Hispanic and youngest judge in the state of New York. As a judge, Sonia's hard work and fair decisions brought her to the attention of President Bill Clinton, who nominated her to the U.S. Court of Appeals. When a seat opened up on the Supreme Court, the highest court in the United States, she was President Barack Obama's first choice.

The ten-year-old girl from the Bronx had made her dreams come true!

CONDOLEEZZA RICE

Condoleezza Rice spent her early years in Birmingham, Alabama. It was the most segregated city in the South, and she often had to deal with racism. Her parents told her that she could do anything—"if she could dream it, she could do it"—and believed that education was the key to success. So Condoleezza studied hard. She also took piano, figure skating, and French lessons.

In her early teens, her family moved to Colorado, and Condoleezza entered the University of Denver at the age of fifteen to study piano. She planned to become a concert pianist, but she wandered into a class on international relations and decided on the spot to change her major to political science. She went on to get a master's degree in economics and a Ph.D. in international studies.

SHOCK WAVES

Condoleezza was eight on September 15, 1963, when a bomb, set by people who were against equal rights for African Americans, exploded at the church where civil rights leaders met. Four young girls, one of them a friend of Condoleezza's, were killed and many others were injured. Condoleezza and her family felt the force of the blast from their home.

SECRETARY OF STATE

SURPRISING CONNECTIONS

The college lecture that got Condoleezza hooked on political science and international relations was taught by Josef Korbel. He was the father of the very first woman to become secretary of state—Madeleine Albright (see "More Amazing Women Who Changed the World," p. 95).

Condoleezza became a professor at Stanford University, but in 1989 she was asked to work for the National Security Council (NSC) under President George H. W. Bush. Condoleezza returned to Stanford at the end of his term as president, but his son, George W. Bush, asked her to come back to Washington when he was elected president. Condoleezza became the first female head of the NSC, and in 2005 was named secretary of state, the first African American woman to hold that job. As secretary of state, she led efforts to promote democracy and peace around the world.

After leaving office in 2009, Condoleezza returned to Stanford and continues to teach there today.

ANN BANCROFT

FACT FILE

★ **BORN:** September 29, 1955, in St. Paul, Minnesota
★ **SPOUSE:** Never married
★ **CHILDREN:** None
★ **DIED:** Still alive

Ann Bancroft's family explored Minnesota's wilderness on camping and canoe trips when she was young. By the time she was eight, Ann was planning camping trips with cousins and friends. In fourth grade, she began camping alone in the family's orchard in the winter, and when she was fourteen, she and her brother **rappeled** down a frozen waterfall.

Ann had a learning disability (see sidebar) and struggled in school, but she did well in sports and made friends. She went to college to become a teacher, and spent four years as a physical and special education teacher before she had a chance to make a childhood dream come true: to join an expedition to the North Pole.

In 1986, Ann set out from an island in the Canadian Arctic, and fifty-six days later she and her teammates reached the North Pole by dogsled. Temperatures were as low as 70 degrees below zero! The team survived on oatmeal, cheese, noodles, dried meat, and fat.

AFRICAN ADVENTURES

After she finished fourth grade, Ann's father joined the Peace Corps and moved the family to Kenya, in Africa, for two years. Ann attended the local public school and had a great time getting to know the people and exploring the new environment.

POLAR EXPLORER

DYSLEXIA

Ann has a learning disability called dyslexia, which makes reading difficult. She believes it was good training for joining a polar expedition. On an expedition, you have to focus on putting one foot in front of the other and doing hard work, which is exactly what people with learning differences have to do every day.

After that, Ann wanted to go on even more adventures. She skied across Greenland, and in 1992 she led three women on an expedition to Antarctica—the South Pole. It took them sixty-seven days to make the 660-mile journey. She returned to Antarctica in 2001 with Norwegian adventurer Liv Arnesen and they became the first women to ski across the frozen continent.

Today, Ann encourages girls to pursue their dreams through money provided by the Ann Bancroft Foundation.

BRRRR...

On her trip to the North Pole, Ann suddenly felt the snow give way underneath her feet, and she fell into freezing polar water. She was able to climb out quickly and change her clothes, or she would have died. It took her two days to stop shivering!

MAYA LIN

FACT FILE

★ **BORN:** October 5, 1959, in Athens, Ohio

★ **SPOUSE:** Daniel Wolf

★ **CHILDREN:** India, Rachel

★ **DIED:** Still alive

Maya Lin always liked to build things. When she was a little girl, she built miniature towns for fun. She also loved to hike.

Maya was good at math, and decided to study **architecture** at Yale. As a college senior, she entered a contest to design a Vietnam veterans memorial in Washington, D.C., and won first prize.

Her design was very different from most war memorials. It was a V-shaped wall in polished black stone with the names of the more than 58,000 American servicemen and women who were killed or missing in Vietnam. Some veterans said it resembled a black scar and felt like it was an insult to them, but Maya always believed it would help people.

When the memorial opened in 1982, the world discovered she was right. More than four million people visit "the Wall" every year.

GIFTS AT THE WALL

Many people leave items at the Vietnam Veterans Memorial for their loved ones. These gifts include medals, combat boots, teddy bears, poems, letters, photos, and even once a motorcycle! The National Park Service collects and takes care of these gifts, and an education center is being built to display them.

ARTIST AND ARCHITECT

REMEMBERING LEWIS AND CLARK

In 2000, Maya was asked to create a series of sculptures to celebrate the two-hundredth anniversary of the Lewis and Clark Expedition. These pieces are installed in parks along the Columbia River in Oregon and Washington and honor the native people, the land, and the explorers.

Maya created more memorials, including a civil rights memorial in Montgomery, Alabama. Then she turned her attention to other kinds of art and architecture. Her sculptures and buildings, inspired by the natural world, can be seen all over the world.

In 2009, Maya started her biggest project. *What Is Missing?* includes a website with videos, sounds, and stories as well as sculptures in the natural world to document the plants, species, and habitats that are being lost. Maya hopes it will inspire people to take better care of the planet.

MICHELLE OBAMA

FACT FILE

★ **BORN:** January 17, 1964, in Chicago, Illinois

★ **SPOUSE:** Barack Obama

★ **CHILDREN:** Malia, Natasha (Sasha)

★ **DIED:** Still alive

Michelle Robinson's family was originally from South Carolina, and her great-great-grandfather was a slave. Michelle was born in Chicago. Her family didn't have a lot of money—four people lived in a one-bedroom home—but her mother and father made sure she and her brother received good educations.

Michelle did well in school, skipped second grade, and went to a special high school for gifted students where she graduated second in her class. She also had a competitive streak and liked to beat her brother, Craig, at games like Monopoly and Chinese checkers. She followed Craig to Princeton University and then went on to Harvard Law School. After graduating, she returned to Chicago to work for a law firm.

The next summer, her law firm asked her to advise a new intern—Barack Obama. Michelle said no when Barack first asked her out on a date, but she later agreed. They were married three years later.

FIRST LADY FIRSTS

Not only is Michelle the first African American First Lady, she is the first First Lady to tweet and to host a Google+ Hangout. In 2013, she became the first First Lady to present an Academy Award.

FIRST LADY, CHILDREN'S HEALTH ADVOCATE

JOINING FORCES

Beginning in 2011, Michelle and Jill Biden, the wife of Vice President Joe Biden, started a program called Joining Forces. The program calls on Americans to support members of the U.S. military, veterans, and their families.

Both Michelle and her husband left the law firm to work in public service. When Barack entered politics and ran for president, Michelle campaigned for her husband and took care of their daughters. People admired both her sense of style and the fact that she always put her family first.

As First Lady, Michelle has been dedicated to inspiring young people to take charge of their futures by getting a good education and giving back to society. Michelle also wants to encourage young people to be healthier. Her Let's Move! program brings together parents, teachers, doctors, and communities to help them make good choices when it comes to diet and exercise. One thing Michelle did to promote better health was to plant a vegetable garden at the White House.

SERENA WILLIAMS

FACT FILE

★ **BORN:** September 26, 1981, in Saginaw, Michigan

★ **SPOUSE:** None

★ **CHILDREN:** None

★ **DIED:** Still living

Before Serena Williams was old enough to hold a racket, her father knew he wanted both her and her older sister Venus to play tennis. Serena was three years old when she first started hitting a tennis ball. The family carried brooms to tennis courts in their hometown of Compton, California, to clean up broken glass and garbage on the neglected courts before they could practice.

When Venus started to compete in tennis matches, Serena wanted to play, too. Her father said she wasn't ready, so Serena secretly entered a tournament for girls ten and younger. She made it all the way to the finals, where Venus defeated her. It was the first of many times that the unstoppable Williams sisters would battle it out for a victory!

Venus and Serena burst onto the professional tennis scene in 1995. The sisters' power and competitive spirit made them stand out, and they brought a colorful style to the court with their splashy outfits. They were also black in a sport largely dominated by white men and women.

MAKING A DIFFERENCE

The Serena Williams Foundation helps young people whose families have been the victims of violent crime. Serena's foundation also builds schools and promotes education worldwide.

TENNIS STAR

SISTER ACT

Serena's tennis career and life are closely tied with those of her older sister Venus. From 1998 to 2015, they played against each other in twenty-six matches. Serena won fifteen of them. Despite their fierce battles on the court, the sisters are close friends. They've even had the chance to combine forces to win thirteen Grand Slam doubles titles!

Serena won her first Grand Slam title (one of the four annual events that are most important in tennis) in 1999. Since then, she's won many more titles despite injuries and the sudden death of her oldest sister, Yetunde. At the same time, Serena proved she's a woman of many talents by becoming an actress and also starting her own clothing line.

Serena's 2015 win at Wimbledon brought her total Grand Slam titles to 21—just one and three, respectively, behind all-time tennis greats Steffi Graf (22) and Margaret Court (24). Will Serena break their records? She's certainly well on her way!

MISTY COPELAND

FACT FILE

★ **BORN:** September 10, 1982, in Kansas City, Missouri

★ **SPOUSE:** Never married

★ **CHILDREN:** None

★ **DIED:** Still alive

Misty Copeland, the first black woman to star in the ballets *Firebird* and *Swan Lake* for the American Ballet Theater, didn't grow up in a community where many little girls took ballet. Her parents separated when she was two, and Misty's mother moved the family to California. Misty loved having five siblings, but the large family meant that her mother struggled to pay the bills and there wasn't always enough food. Misty got through the difficult times by working hard in school. She also loved dancing to Mariah Carey music videos.

Misty's drill team coach suggested she take ballet, and Misty took her first lesson at a Boys & Girls Club when she was thirteen. Most ballerinas begin training much younger than that, usually at the age of five or six, but her ballet teacher saw that Misty had natural talent. Soon, she was dancing every day after school and moved in with her teacher to make it easier to get to her lessons.

PRACTICE, PRACTICE, PRACTICE

It takes a lot of hard work to make it as a professional ballerina: Misty practices for eight hours a day, six days a week!

She may have started late, but Misty was born to be a star. Just five years after her first lesson, Misty joined the American Ballet Theater (ABT), widely considered to be the best ballet company in the United States. But not everyone